D1231723

EVERY **MOTHER** IS A
CEO

EVERY **MOTHER** IS A
CEO

—— Management Lessons from My Mother ——•

DHANJIT VADRA

RUPA

Published by
Rupa Publications India Pvt. Ltd 2022
7/16, Ansari Road, Daryaganj
New Delhi 110002

Sales Centres:
Allahabad Bengaluru Chennai
Hyderabad Jaipur Kathmandu
Kolkata Mumbai

ISBN: 978-93-5520-184-3

First impression 2022

10 9 8 7 6 5 4 3 2 1

The moral right of the author has been asserted.

Printed at Thomson Press India Ltd, Faridabad

To my parents

CONTENTS

FOREWORD

The book you're about to read is a valuable document, an ode to all mothers everywhere and last, but not the least, an illustration of how women and homemakers make excellent managers. I was head of one of India's largest private banks and in my time, my team and I managed to overcome a lot of challenges, but the last couple of years have been unprecedented and extraordinary. In a country like India, after the nationwide lockdown in 2020 due to Covid-19, we saw the more fortunate middle- and upper-classes reduced to working exclusively from home (instead of losing their jobs like the thousands of migrant labourers). And in a society already divided by gender, where women are known to do a majority of unpaid domestic labour, we saw them bravely take on the additional physical and emotional labour for whole families stuck with each other under the same roof, day and night, without rest.

While the division of domestic labour between genders is extremely skewed and unfortunate, this difficult time has also brought to the fore the vital managerial roles women, especially homemakers, play in our daily lives. They are an inspiration. They manage whole households and the well-being of each and every member of their family. From cooking meals, washing clothes, cleaning the house to ensuring the children's homework is done. The story is the same all over the country, the world even. My own wife Smiley has undoubtedly been a pillar of strength for me during this time and opened my eyes to her managerial acumen, making sure my life runs as smoothly as possible.

She has learnt from the best: her dear Bhuai, Urmil Vadra. The author, her son and my brother-in-law, shows us in this book how Urmil Vadra oversaw the blossoming of a formidable business empire and trained her children to live life and work with common sense, guile and compassion. In a deeply personal yet accessible and informative style, this book will tell you the story of a fearless woman and how she brought up her family with efficiency and heart. It also tells us of the many roles Indian housewives play: they are not just homemakers. They are caregivers, supervisors of finances and inventory, educators and HR managers. I hope this story reaches all budding entrepreneurs, students and corporates alike, for they can surely learn a thing or two from this inspiring story, just as I did.

Aditya Puri
Former Managing Director, HDFC Bank
Mumbai, December 2021

INTRODUCTION

This book is dedicated to my mother, Urmil Vadra, who has for over six decades managed our house, raised three children, grandchildren and great-grandchildren, and ensured the well-being of each and every family member and employee through her common-sense management approach. She has also played a crucial supporting role in bringing our business, Allen & Alvan Pvt. Ltd., to where it is today—one of India's largest private hardware manufacturers. My father Devinder Jit Vadra pioneered the decorative brass hardware business in Aligarh and my mother played an essential role in his path-breaking contributions to the business fraternity, economy and society of Aligarh. As the saying goes, behind every successful man, there's a woman. Besides supporting my father, my mother raised a well-adjusted, educated and successful family that has not only excelled in business but in all aspects of life. Now her children have well-settled families of their own, while my father's business, which I eventually took over, has gone from strength to strength.

The skill and finesse with which she has managed our household enterprise rivals that of the best corporate managers across the world. And the ingredients to her method were simple: common-sense, pragmatism, planning and empathy. In this book I would like to lay out my mother's management skills for students, managers and the general reader, in the hope of conveying some unique insights for the corporate world.

৴

Over the last twenty years, various studies[1] have shown that Indian housewives across metros and smaller cities (Tier II—Tier III) have increasingly assumed the role of 'home managers'. They seem to be handling not just the traditional responsibilities of cooking and cleaning but all the affairs of the house from banking duties and bill payments to the children's education and so much more.

---

[1] https://economictimes.indiatimes.com/news/company/corporate-trends/housewives-claim-to-be-smart-managers/articleshow/2190094.cms?from=mdr

This trend is being seen partly as a result of the increasing number of women across big Indian cities and towns who are choosing to get married after graduation, and who consequently feel better equipped to handle challenges greater than their traditional domestic responsibilities. Other factors include changes in the work schedules of a majority of the male workforce—the 9-5 office routine has been replaced by longer work hours since liberalization and the IT boom of the 2000s; the women's desire to contribute to the betterment of their family's lifestyle; and finally, their desire to join the workforce and contribute to the family income.

But the truth is that this is not a recent trend. The indispensable managerial role of Indian women has long been a reality of most Indian households, spanning across the majority of middle- and working-class families, since even before Independence. These women have helmed the Indian household, managed its myriad domestic and caregiving responsibilities without any formal training, only with common sense. A living, breathing example of this fact is my mother, Urmil Vadra. Through the last six decades, Urmil Vadra has educated herself in and practised the art and science of raising a family and running a household with such finesse that all managers would do well to take a leaf out of her book. She has applied operational efficiency, supply-chain management, innovation and long-term thinking in order to maintain the health, wealth and well-being of her family.

My mother hails from the town of Gujarat, now in Pakistan, where she was born in 1935. After Partition her family moved to Jalandhar, where she spent about ten years as the youngest of eleven siblings (she had seven brothers, three sisters). As the youngest child of a huge household, I can't help but imagine that she grew up as a pampered girl. She married my father in 1956 and, after that, moved to Aligarh. In a sense, my father was the polar opposite of my mother—he was the eldest of eight siblings (he had five brothers and three sisters). His family, originally from Sialkot in Pakistan, had come for a summer vacation to Nainital in 1947. Then Partition changed their lives too, and they settled permanently in Aligarh, where they already had a factory Eden & Co. established in 1930 manufacturing locks and hardware.

Her marriage brought, without a doubt, a dramatic transition for my mother—going from the youngest child in the house to being the eldest woman at her in-laws'. A horde of responsibilities now awaited her, even as she acclimatized to the new household. However, she had observed from her own childhood how a big household ought to function. The majority of her new home's management fell on her, as was to be expected at the time. But it is fair to say that she handled this shift admirably. She systematically learned how things functioned in my father's house. Her main responsibilities included supervision of the kitchen and managing the whole family's meals: from getting my father's siblings' school lunches packed to ensuring my grandparents got their food on time. She also supervised the studies of my father's siblings, ensured their clothes were washed and ironed. She was the eldest daughter-in-law—everyone looked up to her for guidance, emotional support and daily sustenance. She became the de-facto peacemaker, breaking up fights and brokering peace between clashing adolescents and teenagers—all the while appearing not to take any sides. In that sense, it was a very delicate position. She had to keep everyone happy, pamper everybody, while also maintaining order and discipline. She also planned picnics and socializing of the family, along with ensuring top-notch hospitality for the visiting sisters-in-law and brothers-in-law in coordination with lady of the house.

Most women have this responsibility thrust on them when they get married, of gauging the workings of their new home and getting used to the family members. My father's family was huge—five brothers, three sisters and his parents. Though it was a little overwhelming for my mother in the beginning, she took inspiration from her own mother, and the latter's hard work and systematic scheduling in keeping a large family fed and happy. In turn, she was supported by my father in whatever she did. They both had each other's back from the very beginning, and this mutual understanding and support continued to grow when they had children and became parents. This was crucial in the times to come.

∿

'There come to us moments in life when about some things we need no proofs from without. A little voice within us tells us, "You are on the right track, move neither to your left nor right, but keep to the straight and narrow way."'

—MAHATMA GANDHI

Some years into my parents' marriage came a watershed moment. It was one of those points in people's lives which they look back on and realize that it changed everything. At that time my grandfather, Sant Ram Vadra, had a flourishing locks business in Aligarh. But then my father decided to strike out on his own and make a name for himself, thus changing the course of our family's life. I can only imagine the challenges and anxieties my parents must have faced, as they left behind their settled, comfortable life in a big house full of servants and family to look after them and their one-year-old infant (myself), and travelled to a new city, the capital New Delhi, to start over. As I understand it now, this was a move motivated by the family dynamics, and my father's need to prove his mettle by starting over from scratch. Most importantly, through all this upheaval, my mother unstintingly supported his vision.

Not long after, I had a sister. We lived in a flat in Rajinder Nagar. Although my parents eventually came back to Aligarh after two years, my father would not have gained the business knowledge and experience necessary (away from the shelter of family) to eventually set up the fledgling empire we have now. And certainly none of this would have been possible without the support of my mother.

My father was a very hard-working man with several academic degrees, including an LLM, which he got before he joined his father's business, and before his marriage. He had wanted to be a lawyer initially. He even apprenticed for a while with a practicing lawyer in Delhi.

My mother, however, intuitive as she is, knew that entrepreneurship was in his blood. Recognizing his ambition and potential, she gently nudged him towards the path of business. Business was in my father's destiny and with my mother's encouragement, he eventually realized he had to work for himself. In Delhi, my father tried to establish a brass foundry enterprise. My grandfather already had a factory manufacturing locks and hinges in Aligarh since 1930. My father aimed to expand the business into other product lines and to prove to the family that he could stand on his own, he set up his own operations in Delhi in 1958. However, he had to keep travelling back to Aligarh, since the product was sourced from there.

After a couple of years, when things in the capital did not quite take off as expected, my father decided to return to his hometown and eventually founded what is today one of India's largest private hardware manufacturers. He managed to achieve all this by taking innumerable scouting trips abroad, following his intuitions about India's strengths including the low cost of skilled labour, and ultimately becoming one of the first people to export such hardware goods to Africa and Europe. He was successful in convincing clients about the quality of his product and its timely delivery. With his diplomacy and business savvy, he convinced clients all over the world to extend letters of credit, and built a reputation of a dependable exporter of quality goods.

The business was also able to grow because my parents had worked on their own relationship, on building complete trust in one another, so they did not need to look outside for approval and support. It is this strong foundation that allowed them to coordinate and work as a unit. They wholeheartedly backed each other's instincts and forged a strong partnership that was able to navigate the crucial, make-or-break moments of life—and business.

My mother was there at each and every one of the vital junctures in our family's life. She helped manage the business, as well as our big household—there were eleven in the immediate family, along with a rotating cast of cousins and aunts who came to stay in our house for extended periods. One could say that the prosperity of both were interlinked, and the thriving of one helped the other. And it was Urmil Vadra's able hands at the helm. From their time in Delhi, my father had grown to trust her judgement because of her common-sense approach to household management and her unstinting emotional and even financial support. So, he handed the responsibility of the bank lockers and the factory to her. This was a very big endorsement of his faith in her management skills.

∽

My mother looked after everything in our house, from the kitchen to the children's education, and even our social position in Aligarh. Our personal and social lives were shaped by her with grace, as she planned the construction of our home in a prime location, hosted the local Inner Wheel and Rotary Club meetings and entertained guests with her easy sense of humour and without indulging in frivolous gossiping. After we came back from Delhi my mother was the provider, she was the one who organized everything. She supervised our meals and prepared us for school, all the while keeping the house in order vis-à-vis cleaning, food inventory, maintenance work, finances, managing the in-laws, the staff and so on. There were also guests dropping in all the time, especially during holidays every few months. I remember once we drove to Kashmir and stayed in a Dal Lake houseboat for a whole month! It was a smooth and thoroughly enjoyable vacation, all planned and managed by my mother. From provisions for the long cross-country drive to having our meals and games in place on the houseboat, she left no stone unturned. And even though they had to step out of the houseboat for a while, they returned with all the nutritious local food such as cherries and apples, along with the famous water from the Chashme Shahi spring, known for its digestive properties. They even took us to the Rotary Club functions, where no other parents brought their children because of the prohibitive cost of food—they believed that their children had much to learn from such social events and moreover they loved us and tried to take us with them wherever they could.

Aside from her daily tasks, my mother also planned for the long-term future of the family. She took it upon herself to keep track of the education of her three children. She researched the most reputed schools and made sure that each of us went to the best of them. Both my sisters were sent to Welham's boarding school, Dehradun. My education was mainly in Aligarh, as my parents wanted me to learn the ropes of the business from the ground up, and eventually take over. Mother was present throughout our academic lives, constantly engaging with our teachers and our studies, which was rewarding for her as all her three children turned out to be University gold medalists.

Besides academics, she took on the responsibility for our moral and financial education, teaching us how to handle money, to respect the people working for us and so on. As we all know, institutions are not the only places where children acquire knowledge. Countless studies have shown that the most important education happens at home. The development of personality, moral character and habits can shape children into healthy, well-adjusted and successful adults or maladjusted, temperamental also-rans. Our parents, especially our mother, did not coddle us, nor did they shame us in public for our mistakes. They taught us right from wrong, how to treat people, how to save money, how to shop smartly and so much more. When we did do something wrong, they told us in private, instead of scolding us in front of friends or teachers, always careful that we didn't lose our respect and dignity with a public reprimand. Above all, our mother loved us, and was unwilling to lose her children's goodwill under the pretext of discipline. This had a positive effect on us, and as a family we have now adopted this approach in our social and business dealings. We are who we are because of our mother's efforts at shaping us into confident human beings.

∿

My mother's focus on character building and morality strengthened the bonds of the whole family and our place in society. Clients, employees and acquaintances trusted us. Undoubtedly, this helped in crafting our family's image as a business even as we became a prosperous household. Mother's relentless ambition and flawless execution when it came to managing our reputation took our standing to the next level. She was one of the first people in Aligarh who decided on the construction of a massive new house, at a time when most middle- and upper-middle-class homes were renovated Nawabi havelis or smaller kothis on 200-300 sq. yard plots.

This was an unusual but insightful move by my mother—she was fearless and welcomed change, setting an example for everyone. The physical building of our house became a symbol of our family's strength and prosperity.

She was undaunted by a challenge, and this spirit was soon to reflect in the business. My father was the first to build a state-of-the-art hardware manufacturing factory in Aligarh, at a time when people thought large factories were not feasible as they required too much maintenance. It was my mother who supported this idea too, and stood firmly behind him.

∽

How was my mother able to accomplish all of these things? This is not an easy question to answer. As the great business tycoon Dhirubhai Ambani once said, 'If you work with determination and with perfection, success will follow.' I believe my mother had large reserves of both. In the following pages I will attempt to elaborate on her methods and strategies by sharing observations, memories and anecdotes from her life. Essentially, she has, through the experience of caring for the family and living her own life well, mastered the basic but crucial skills for effective management: time management, planning, inventory management, financial

management and people management. I will deal with each
of these skills in the following chapters and hope my mother's
management style can be a template for students, managers
and entrepreneurs out there.

1

TIME MANAGEMENT

"Time is the most valuable coin in your life. You and you alone will determine how that coin will be spent. Be careful that you do not let other people spend it for you."

—CARL SANDBURG

These words by a renowned American poet have rung true for decades, and will continue to do so for human endeavours for all time. For entrepreneurs and businesses, setting up and running small-, medium- or large-scale enterprises requires a judicious use of time. Time is the agent of history and progress; it is one of our most important resources. To make the most efficient use of our time, management and self-help theories repeatedly emphasize the priority of planning our work according to the goals we want to achieve. In other words, it is crucial to make sure that time is on our side.

At a practical level, for the most effective time management strategy one should first identify their goals and priorities, evaluate the time available, log the time spent in the necessary work, then develop a plan and keep cross-checking goals against the progress made, adjusting the plans accordingly. This feedback loop plays a big part in optimizing organizational strategies.

꒒

However, the very first step for achieving anything, as countless business gurus will tell you, is: desire. Napoleon Hill, the bestselling author of *Think and Grow Rich*, shows us how with the perfect example. He demonstrates the 'secret' behind the success of the automobile czar Henry Ford through an oft-repeated anecdote: Ford conceived his vision for the famous V8 engine (the first engine with all eight cylinders cast in one single block) many years before it was actually produced. At first, his engineers believed it could only exist on paper.

'Produce it anyway,' he told them. 'But, it's impossible,' they replied. 'Go ahead,' he commanded them to keep at it. A whole year went by as the engineers worked hard to achieve their target, but they were unsuccessful.

When Ford checked in with them after a year, they told him it was impossible, and he replied, 'Go right ahead. I want it, and I'll have it.' They went ahead, and then, as if by a miracle, they figured it out! Ford's persistence won out in the end. Henry Ford knew what he wanted, wouldn't take no for an answer and kept going at it. And eventually, following this most basic but crucial principle for achieving anything in life, he succeeded.

Now, my mother is no Henry Ford. She did not revolutionize modern mass production and change the way the world moved. But in her role as a loving, dutiful mother and wife, she knew exactly what she wanted: she was driven by her innate desire to see her family thrive. She wanted the best, most fulfilling life for her family; this was why she worked day and night, tirelessly, towards this goal. She even used her household tips and tricks to bring about a positive change in our business management. With her persistence, she oversaw a hardware manufacturing empire grow from infancy to dizzying heights through two generations, raised responsible, bright and well-rounded children who now have kids of their own, as well as groomed domestic staff with compassion and rigour who maintain the household and the factory with utmost efficiency.

∿

As a mother, her own happiness was always related to her family's well-being. But even though she knew her ultimate goal from the beginning, she didn't have an army of engineers or helpers to assist her with her myriad tasks every day, or a retinue of assistants to plan for our long-term future. So how did she manage it all?

She was a master of time management. My mother has lived her life by the motto 'a stitch in time saves nine'. She would be up every day at six without fail, have her customary cup of tea and then launch into a rush of activity—getting the ball rolling in the kitchen, turning on the milk churner to make fresh butter, supervising breakfast preparations, managing grocery supplies, getting the kids ready for school, packing delicious and nutritious lunches for us and our father, getting the clothes washed and ironed and so on. She would be done with everything by eleven o'clock. She would then visit the factory for two-three hours, dipping her hand in the management, maintaining some files, helping my father out while giving him some much-needed company at work. My father was a dedicated workaholic, who rarely took Sundays off. When my mother spent time at the factory with him, chatting and helping him out with a few things, my father relaxed. With his batteries recharged, he would return to work with a renewed focus. Sometimes he consulted my mother on business matters that were on his mind, and my mother would respond—despite her lack of management training—and give advice according to her own understanding, based on her expertise in managing the myriad functions of the household. My parents kept each other company this way.

This also helped in keeping the atmosphere in the workplace casual. Not so casual so as to let people fall behind in work, but there was no strict, 'stiff-upper-lip' management. As long as the work got done, people were allowed flexible timings, casual dress code, etc. This helped build team morale and created a collaborative and enriching work culture, and most importantly, increased productivity and incentive.

My mother's workday did not end when she came back from the factory. There was still much to be done. We have a large family, both my parents have eight-ten siblings. My father being the eldest, there were always relatives and cousins dropping in. As children my sisters and I were taught to welcome cousins and guests with a smile. We were taught to give smiles, not take them. Throughout her time in-charge, my mother ensured that arrangements for food, snacks and general hospitality for guests were always in place. Guests could comfortably stay in our house for up to a month, and would be surprised by the extravagant variety of food served daily, be it sumptuous halwas or savoury chaats, hot samosas or plates of noodles. That there has never been a shortage of anything at home is a feat that my mother single-handedly achieved through her intuitive management. The manager of the house kept the kitchen and the house stocked for any eventuality and treated all guests with grace and love, whether they were relatives staying with us or acquaintances who had come over for tea.

Even when there were no guests, there would always be buttermilk, or *matha*, freshly made every morning in the house and served to everyone, including the household staff. When I started working, she would send a flask with me to the factory, for myself and my office staff. 'If you're going, just take this with you,' she would say. She always had an eye for details like this, the small things that make a big difference. Before management gurus coined the term 'empathetic leadership', my mother was practising it all along. Most importantly, she taught me, through her household techniques and gestures, how to manage people and keep them happy. For instance, she kept aside Diwali gifts for employees even if they had gone back home for the festival. If the sweets went bad, she found other thoughtful gifts like clothes and various household items. She also carefully managed to avoid favouritism among the household staff, e.g. if a guest gave *baksheesh*, or a tip, to the cook and the cleaner she made sure that the gardener also got an equal tip. So all the staff was kept motivated and happy.

At the end of the workday, when the worker responsible for locking up our factory came home to hand over the keys, mother always made it a point to offer him something to eat or drink. She was always gracious and our staff member looked forward to meeting her, greeting her with a *namaste*, and was conscientious about his responsibility of locking up carefully. Till date I have not had any problems with this seemingly small, but extremely important part of our workplace security. And I have learned so much from watching both my mother and father manage people with finesse, that I have tried to adopt this approach in my own management of the factory.

Taking a cue from my parents, I've made sure to maintain a light atmosphere in the factory, and developed a rapport with my team through humour. Humour plays an important role, though understated in management textbooks, in keeping up the morale of the workforce. If you bring a smile or two to your colleagues, it does no harm. In fact, within limits, it enhances the atmosphere of work, along with productivity. A tense workplace cultivates fear, fatigue and resentment—all detrimental to morale and productivity. So I always make it a point to joke around with the workers, keep their spirits up, bring smiles to the team so everyone is relaxed and able to give their best performance.

✓

Coming back to time management. According to the famous '1 Billion-Dollar Morning Routine', allegedly followed by star billionaires like Elon Musk, after waking up you're supposed to meditate, exercise, practise journaling, make to-do lists and read, along with a host of other self-care activities in order to *prepare* yourself for the day and ur *actual* tasks. They say that if you follow this regimen you will be as productive as the most successful people in the world.

I have seen people try out this routine on YouTube, with varying results. However, what is most striking to me, when I compare this with my mother's routine, is that by the time people get done with the 15-odd activities in the 'billionaire routine', my mother is done with the majority of her work for the day! She doesn't spend half her morning exclusively doing 'self-care' activities. In fact, it is during the busy morning time when she coordinates breakfast, lunch, clothes and prepares everyone else for the upcoming workday that she manages to squeeze in her own personal morning routine—that's all the self-care and self-hygiene she needs. Not a moment to lose.

The energy, dedication and focus she has had for decades leaves most tycoons' and experts' theories in the shade. It's not just the amount of work she gets done, but her eye for detail that is unique. I'll share another example: the other day she was teaching me how to fry fish and she let me in on a secret. If you're right-handed and after frying you take the fish out from the left side of the pan, you are able to drain more oil out, rather than taking it out from the right side of the pan. Try it! This is a simple yet profound piece of insight that no book or recipe will ever tell you. And it saves you much time and effort. She has picked up such tips from her own experience, years and years of practice, trial and error, and shared them with me. Through this, she reminds me of another lesson she has drilled into us since the beginning: whatever you do, do it well. Else there's no point in even trying. This is a much-overlooked lesson in strategy and organization—one cannot consistently aim for optimum results without paying attention to the small details. Ambition is complimented by mindfulness.

ᔕ

Let us now consider a hypothetical. Laxman is the head of sales at an organization. He has been a top performer of his team and always finds opportunities even in a crisis. Due to his unparalleled performance, the management has immense faith in him and continues to set high targets for him. On the other hand, fellow team members continue to push unprofitable products with minimal effort while escaping the management's oversight. With rising expectations, Laxman has to take on more responsibility while the rest of the team is content to coast and stick to their underperforming product lines. Laxman is happy with the management's faith in his abilities but is finding himself stretched thin. The increasing workload and the management's blind eye to underperforming and unhelpful colleagues are taking a toll. How can he plan, multi-task and meet targets in such a stressful situation?

There would have to be a strong, personal motivation for Laxman to continue performing in this environment. It could be that the products were his own brainchild and he had a personal stake in their success. Or perhaps a promotion or partnership promised by the management. This would secure his family's future, his children's education and future medical expenses. Motivation, the personal stake a manager or an employee has in the business, is key.

In my mother's case, the motivation was extremely

personal, and ever present. Her connection with my father and us children was one of pure love. This was the foundation of our relationship as a family. My mother was, and still is, committed to our future and well-being. Some people might say that this is why you can't compare running a business with running a house. No employee or manager can have as much personal investment in the business as a mother can in her 'enterprise'. Nevertheless, it is this motivation that allowed her to plan her day and fit into it all the activities that took care of the physical, emotional and educational needs of our family.

I believe that this is *exactly* why we must look up to homemakers such as my mother as case studies for managers, students and entrepreneurs. How can we invest into management the profound meaning that housework holds for homemakers? If this question can be answered then the next crucial question about multitasking can be answered too. If your complete happiness, survival and self-actualization is dependent on the well-being of your organization (or family), then you will through sheer instinct and experience develop strategies for multitasking, meeting the various needs of different clients, planning short-term tasks as well as taking steps for the future, long-term security. However, we all know that employees only have a limited stake in an enterprise, as opposed to business owners. But my mother's compassionate and common-sense management approach shows that by creating a genial and incentivized workplace environment, filled with positive reinforcement and not constant surveillance, can foster a deeper connection between employees, their roles and the management—thus leading to higher productivity and innovation. In other words, if employees are made to feel like they are part of a community, they will necessarily be empowered and moved to perform, innovate and achieve efficiency in their roles.

∿

My mother has also been an active member of the society, as part of social clubs like the International Inner Wheel Club for women, and the ladies wing of the Rotary Club. And so, the second half of her carefully scheduled day was usually occupied with these engagements. She usually spent it planning events and hosting tea and other parties for the social communities that she was part of. She would host one or more of these gatherings every fortnight, and needless to say, they were perfect in execution and hospitality, leaving no stone unturned and no guest unsatisfied. This included conceiving elaborate menus, tactful guest lists, and immaculate décor complimenting the crockery. Due to her graceful hosting skills, guests always felt welcome and taken care of, and never rushed for dinner if they were enjoying a drink—each guest felt as if he was the most important invitee. Both parties of an ongoing social feud were never invited to the same event, it was always a colourful mix of people who enlivened the atmosphere and kept things jovial and easy. The children were always fed early along with the chauffeurs. Almost all these events ended with guests going out of their way to thank their host.

Despite these social commitments—some hosted at home while others attended outside—my mother was always there for us when we came back from school, whether we were returning from kindergarten or from an MBA class. If she had a meeting around that time, she would make sure to inform us in advance and keep some food prepared for us at home. When she came back home she had many stories to tell. We would gather around her and she would recount all the funny incidents and drama from her social gatherings. Then she made sure dinner was ready by 7.30 pm. She never let us go to sleep on an empty stomach. If we were too tired after playtime in the evenings, she would wake us up and insist we eat before tucking us into bed.

By organizing her routine and responsibilities around our sustenance, and with caregiving as her primary objective, my mother was able to devote quality time to all. Not just us kids, but my father, our domestic staff and the factory employees were taken care of, and this meant that *they* performed well in their jobs and responsibilities. It not only ensured that everyone around was well nourished, it allowed her to develop a well-rounded approach to the business of life. Her meticulousness was not just limited to our daily sustenance, but also long-term planning for our education, business and future lives. In a later chapter we will discuss the aspects of long-term planning that she was able to pull off, which helped us prosper in all areas of life. And in conclusion, one can say that if you have the core interests of everyone involved with your business at heart—that is if people are treated with compassion and are not just a means to an end for you—you can find ways to manage your time and chart a definite path to success.

⌢

An efficient manager is able to envision their business as a functioning, intricate ecosystem. Components in this ecosystem are further connected to other external networks. The manager's job is to keep track of all the links, for the efficient functioning of the whole. The larger 'business' is a *gestalt* that relies on the efficient functioning of each constituent part. Too little (or too much) focus on any single component will disrupt the balance and bring the whole system down. This is why time management is important, to give appropriate attention to each task, keeping in mind the short- and long-term objectives. My mother's intuitive and well-honed strategies to efficiently manage time, then, are lessons in the practical art of balance.

2

PLANNING

'In preparing for battle I have always found that plans are useless, but planning is indispensable.'

—DWIGHT D. EISENHOWER

What is life, if not a battle? A battle against forces like the economy, society, climate? The world, such as it is now, is a place of adversity for human beings; and the only way one can protect their loved ones and ensure their prosperity and happiness is to plan in advance for their long-term future. Nobody knew this better than Eisenhower, the legendary military officer and president f the United States of America, who supervised the invasions of France and Germany during World War 2, and as president of his country oversaw unprecedented economic prosperity for his people.

Planning, in life as well as management, is one of the most powerful and effective ways to attain what we want. Nobody plans to fail; they simply fail to plan. In other words, *failing to plan is akin to planning to fail.* Just think about it: if you travel, you plan your trip. If you are getting married, you plan your wedding. If you throw a party, you plan the event. You would not dream of doing any of these things without some measure of prior planning. So how is living a life of success filled with meaning, happiness and fulfilment any different? Every evening my father had his cup of tea and discussed business plans with my mother. Every day they earmarked targets for savings and future expenditures. For instance, when they finally built the factory, it was not huge—it was scaled only to meet their requirements and had realistic production capacity. This soon allowed them to build an adjoining office. They did not accumulate unserviceable debts (creating a 'white elephant'), always planned within their means while keeping all stakeholders in mind (e.g. investing in PF schemes for all employees).

Planning your life, or business, is equivalent to having a road map that helps you reach your destination. Unless you have already been to the place you want to go many times and know just how to get there, you need a good map. Is it not foolish to get in your car and drive around aimlessly, hoping to eventually reach your destination?

When you take the time to plan your life, you are taking the steps necessary to not only identify and reach your goal, but to do so in the most efficient manner. Rather than relying on pure chance, a life plan details the exact route you need to take. It helps you get there in the shortest time possible without running out of fuel.

Planning can be applied to both small and big aspects of our lives or business. It can be for the short- or the long-term. Perhaps you want to perform better at your job, or get a promotion, or save up enough for a marriage or your children's education, or be an efficient manager, or grow your business. The possibilities are endless, depending on our desires.

Planning gives us a clear perspective on what our desires and goals are, what needs to be done to achieve them, and in some cases, the amount of time or resources we should spend towards their fulfilment. Remember, planning is not about charting shortcuts, but about finding the most realistic path to your goal.

ゝ

The importance of planning in management cannot be overstated. It helps in resource optimization: how and where to allocate resources, how to avoid wastage; setting targets for growth; managing risks and unforeseen challenges; improving human resource management and work culture; and gaining advantage over competitors. Essentially, planning is the nucleus of management activities.

The incredible story of Ardeshir Godrej, founder of the Godrej Group and a pioneering inventor, businessman and thorough patriot, gloriously demonstrates the value of planning. His biography *Vijitmata: Pioneer-Founder Ardeshir Godrej* (2004) tells us the extraordinary story of Godrej's determination, strong sense of right and wrong, and his unflinching loyalty towards something bigger than himself—the nation. Around the turn of the last century, when the British ruled India and nobody trusted Indian products, Ardeshir Godrej revolutionized Indian industry by starting a successful indigenous business and challenging the colonial British empire.

He aimed to manufacture top quality surgical instruments at a time when only imported instruments were considered safe and the British had a stranglehold on the entire surgical instruments market. When his old family friend and investor, Merwanji, wondered if this was a profitable business idea, Godrej said he wanted to first prove that Indians were capable of making sophisticated instruments; after establishing himself in that line, he would move towards manufacturing other, higher selling products.

He worked day and night, sharpening, fashioning, shaping scalpels, forceps, pincers, scissors and other implements for surgery. The enterprise looked promising but when the British proprietor refused to market Godrej's creations as 'Made-in-India', citing the prevailing bias for imported instruments, Godrej backed out. Crestfallen but unwilling to compromise on his principles, he decided to look elsewhere.

After much searching, lightning struck! Recent news had pointed to the increasing burglaries in Bombay, and the police commissioner's warnings about the need for greater security measures. It was then that he realized the great demand for secure locks. Through his research he found that there were many locks in the market of varying qualities, but none that was absolutely secure. So he decided to make *the* unpickable lock.

But he had run out of money from his previous venture. He called on his benefactor, Merwanji, and apologized for being unable to return his loan. Then he told him the whole story, how his instruments had impressed the chemists and the proprietor wanted to market them but under a British name, which he could not agree to. Despite his failure, Merwanji was impressed by his manufacturing and organizational capabilities.

So Godrej pitched his next venture to manufacture locks, better than the ones available in the market. Merwanji asked if he had a plan and an estimate of how much capital he would need. With Merwanji's renewed confidence in him, Godrej revealed his plan: calling skilled workers from Gujarat and Malabar, setting up a workshop at Lalbaug (he had already scouted a suitable location with extra land for expansion), scoping out the competition (he realized Indian locks were crude, handmade and labour-intensive) and training his workers in using technology instead of hands.

Having impressed Merwanji with his detailed research and plan of action, he availed some start-up capital and got to work on manufacturing 'absolutely unpickable' high-security locks, which was the birth of the iconic Anchor brand. Godrej went on to make several ingenious improvements in the industry. First, he cleared misconceptions among the public about the security of locks, such as the idea that the price of a lock depends on the number of levers. Then he reversed the usual process of lock manufacturing by making locks to fit machine-cut keys, instead of the other way around—to ensure their unpickability. Further, realizing the problem of springs even in imported locks, he invented the springless lock! This was the earliest of the thirty-six Godrej patented inventions.

Once he had his product, Godrej had to market it. When the British newspapers refused to carry his advertisements which claimed his locks 'were as good as the imported variety', he went to the nationalist newspapers instead. He also printed and distributed handbills—explaining in matter-of-fact language the process and quality of his manufacturing operation—in the thousands to make everyone in Bombay, and later the whole country, aware of his new wonder lock.

Godrej went on to expand his business, and through extensive research, interminable discussions with his engineers and *mistris*, he made unbreakable and fire-resistant safes, soaps made out of vegetable oils (instead of animal fats, as was the practice in most countries at the time) and filed countless other patents. In addition to studying his competition closely in order to make superior quality products, Godrej also made sure that they were marketed with a flair that was previously unseen. To prove that his safes were truly fire-resistant, he actually burned one of his safes in a public demonstration. In another incident to prove the defects of expensive foreign-made safes, he broke open a wealthy Bombay mill agent's safe, thereby further improving the perception of locally manufactured products.

Isn't it remarkable? At a time when the country was under foreign rule, the intrepid Ardeshir Godrej, motivated by his love for his homeland and armed with meticulous planning, managed to build an empire right under the oppressor's nose! He did thorough research, picking out crucial gaps in the market, toiled day and night to come up with a superior product—and then pulled out all stops in marketing it. Throughout all this, he kept sight of his original goal: self-reliance and self-respect for the nation. He earned praise from the leading luminaries of India at the time, including Rabindranath Tagore, Dr. Annie Besant and Mahatma Gandhi, among others. Godrej's story is an important and inspiring lesson for all.

But you don't need to be a world-famous military commander, the leader of the free world, a pioneering inventor or a hotshot CEO to plan well and succeed. People from all walks of life, especially the housewives of India, are possibly the greatest unsung planners of our time. Managing the daily physical and emotional sustenance of their family, creating conditions for the prosperity of their children and spouses, is one of their most overlooked achievements. Their foresight, dedication and meticulousness in planning their family's lives are unparalleled, and should be studied by all managers. My mother is one of these heroes.

She too was gifted with immense foresight and the

23

gumption to chalk out a road map for our success. First and foremost, her primary loyalty was towards something bigger than herself—not the nation as in Godrej's case—but her family. It was her family's well-being and prosperity that guided all her actions as the manager of our household. She had the capacity to look far ahead into the future, which allowed her to make or facilitate key decisions regarding our family business, her children's education and our home, and work towards them. These decisions have proved to be crucial in our overwhelming success and prosperity— as both a business as well as a thriving family. Some of them include making sure her children were admitted to the best schools: my sisters in Welham's boarding school in Dehradun; I was sent to Lady Fatima Senior Secondary School in Aligarh; she (along with my father) also took up our moral and social education at home, through bedtime stories and instilling in us values of dignity of labour and respect for others, among others. A great example of her financial planning was when she invested in the Reserve Bank of India's (RBI) gold scheme. Now she has got it all back with the RBI's stamp, certifying and even increasing its value.

Our family came back from Delhi to finally resettle in Aligarh, after my father's business did not quite take off. He made the decision, with my mother's support, to start anew, armed with lessons from his own venture to take over the family business in the late 1960s. Despite not hitting the jackpot in Delhi, my father gained a new-found credibility within the family. He had proved his mettle by going out on his own, knowing why and how he failed and having a road map for success on his home turf. Back in Aligarh, my mother had to not only plan our daily sustenance, but also give her inputs on business problems and strategies shared by my father. In fact, as I mentioned earlier, she was the one who pushed him into business in the first place after realizing his deep desire for it.

In Aligarh, our factory premises were initially taken on rent, and the set-up was not very big. But my parents were forward-thinking and eventually they bought the property, along with a big plot next to it. My mother crucially supported my father in this decision, both morally as well as putting her own financial position on the line. She stood firm in her belief of her husband's business acumen and was prepared to sink all her assets, including precious heirlooms, into the venture—and boy did it all pay off handsomely! At that time, people did not see the need for building large manufacturing facilities in Aligarh, and there weren't many businesses that were into quality manufacturing in the city. But my parents had the foresight, which included their intuition as well as knowledge accumulated from their extensive travels and business research, to buy enough land so that the factory could eventually be expanded. As business grew over the first two decades, we ended up expanding and built a new factory in 1990.

If you look around now, Aligarh probably has about 2,000 factories. People have slowly begun to see the importance of state-of-the-art facilities, which help in producing better quality products. But these other factories are relatively smaller in size, and the precedent for their success was set by my father. But my mother was always there behind him throughout all the crucial make-or-break moments, always being mindful of the future. They had, just like Ardeshir Godrej, the nose for success and planning for the future.

Let us break down the thinking behind this. Suppose you're planning to start a business and your estimates show that you require about 5,000 sq. feet of factory land to start. What if you were to buy a 15,000 sq. foot plot instead? Why would you need more land, you ask? As we have seen from the above two examples, if you enter a business with stellar research and make sure to produce superior quality products, your business *will* need to expand. Instead of buying more land later, at an even higher premium, you can spend some more money now and get a 15,000 sq. foot plot. Even though it might cost you more in the beginning, ultimately it is going to supplement many things. Your cost of expansion is going to be minimal. In our case, we not only expanded our state-of-the-art facility many times over and kept up with our growing business, but we now have excess land on which we grow mustard and other vegetables. This produce is distributed amongst the employees too, not just utilized in our kitchen. Land is a versatile resource, it can never go to waste and always yields many benefits when used and cared for properly.

My parents' approach towards property also came into play while setting up our family home. After settling into the business back in Aligarh, my parents decided to build a new house. My mother insisted that our home be situated on the main road in full view of the society, and not inside a gully of some obscure neighbourhood. So, she got our house built on an acre of land in the nice, posh neighbourhood of Civil Lines in Aligarh. It was situated on the main road, which was called Sammat Road, a name later given by my father. According to my mother's vision, it was only proper that our new home be located in a prominent, visible location, so as to project an image of credit-worthiness. Everyone could see a house at a prominent location in a posh area, and keep up with the goings-on from outside. In a small town this helps to keep up appearances and gives protection against vicious gossip-mongers spinning tales about the state of various families and businesses. There were also other, practical reasons, such as ease of access for family members, visitors as well as clients.

It took three-four years to build the house. The construction was supervised entirely by my mother. She stood every day at the spot and had the house made in front of her vigilant eyes. She would go to the site every single day, check on the daily progress and settle the accounts of all the labourers herself. All the payments were made by her and the records maintained by her. We shifted into the house in 1972 and thus, through her vision, started our innings in town as a respectable business family.

People would stand outside and remark at the bold architecture. They said to my parents: *your kids are young, why do you need such a big house?* Our clients from abroad asked my parents: *why don't you build a house in Delhi? It will fetch you more money.* But a house was more than just a business investment for my parents. It was a home for our family. My father loved Aligarh. He believed that one should respect the place where you stay, so he built his house here, at my mother's insistence, instead of building it in a big city like Delhi.

At the time, at least two well-off business families in

Aligarh and Moradabad had built huge houses in Delhi and kept only smaller dwellings here. Every weekend, they would promptly run off to the capital. Eventually having lost all touch with the local community, these people were rooted out of their own hometowns. In fact, one of the big business families in Aligarh lost their fortune because they were spending too much time in Delhi. With no one to look after their business, they kept losing money. Moreover, the next generation was not interested in coming back, so their business eventually shut down.

My parents turned this metropolitan thinking on its head. They built a magnificent house in Aligarh and a smaller one in Delhi. It was our mother's decision to have a base in Aligarh, which gave our family the foundation to build a rich life, connected to our native land, and allowed my father to build and grow a business here. It also told the business fraternity and larger society that we were here to stay.

Even for our house, my mother made sure that we got an extra plot of land. With the excess space, she cultivated a huge kitchen garden. And this had nothing to do with sending a message to society or our status—that was not the point. It is always good to keep an eye on the future, and certain things when planned well, whether by design or luck, turn out to be core benefits. Now we have a thriving kitchen garden and hardly ever have to buy vegetables! She also has plants like turmeric and aanvla, which bring my mother great joy. She spends time pruning and cultivating the plants in her garden every single day, nourishing them so that they in turn can nourish her family.

Finally, the third example of my mother's long-term planning can be seen in our, her children's, education. As we all know, education is not just about imparting basic knowledge, it shapes character and facilitates socialization of students by bringing them into contact with peers from various backgrounds. My mother made sure that we were sent to the best schools. I remained in Aligarh and studied at Lady Fatima Senior Secondary School, as my parents wanted me to eventually take over the family business. After school I did an MBA from the renowned Aligarh Muslim University in town. Both my sisters, on the other hand, were sent to Welham's boarding school in Dehradun as soon as they were eligible. My mother was very progressive in her thinking, about where the girls should study and her emphasis on education. Nobody had even heard of Welham's in a small town like Aligarh, much less thought of sending their girls far away from home for school. Moreover, it's always difficult for parents to live away from their children, but the future of her daughters was more important for her than her personal need to live close to them. My mother played an active role in our studies too, always keeping up with our progress and staying in touch with our teachers.

At home, outside the classroom, she taught us vital life lessons through playful bedtime stories and fables. Once she told us the story of a man who used to go to the river every day. One day he met the river spirit. Seeing his devotion to the river, the spirit said, 'I grant you one wish.'

The man thought for a minute and replied, 'Can I please go home and think about it? I will come back tomorrow.'

'Sure, come back tomorrow,' the spirit said.

The man went back home and asked his wife what she wanted.

'I want gold,' she said.

Then he asked his mother what she wanted.

'I want to see again, I want my sight to be restored,' said his blind mother.

As for himself, the man knew that he had always pined for a son. He kept turning these thoughts over in his mind and went to sleep.

The next day he got up and went back to the river.

'What is your wish?' the river spirit asked.

'I wish for my old mother to see her grandson eating out of gold vessels,' said the man, finally. His wish was granted.

In one stroke, the man combined all three wishes, so his whole family could be happy. Through this story my mother taught us that one must think carefully before speaking, consider all possibilities, and the well-being of everyone involved. This not only helped me in school, but it's a lesson I have carried with myself into business as well. It has helped me deal with clients, suppliers, customers and employees. It taught me to phrase my words in a way that they carried the appropriate weight and achieved desired results. For instance, while negotiating with buyers, I can make them agree to two terms: if they insist on delivery of goods within 30 days, I agree to it on the condition that they release the letter of credit (which is otherwise very difficult to get). I lock in both things, so payment for my order is ensured and delivery schedule fixed. If a buyer is unsure, I guarantee an attractive price—if the order is placed immediately.

Mother also made sure we never missed a single day of school. We were always regular and up to date, which helped maintain our academic performance. As a result, between her three children, we collected five gold medals from the Aligarh Muslim University during our higher studies.

The discipline that I imbibed by being regular and dedicatedly showing up every day—be it for school, college or work—has shaped my entire life. My mother has worked almost every day of her adult life for our family. My father too barely took any days off. Then why should I? This has helped me stay on track with production targets, supply deadlines, client interactions and almost every other aspect of business.

I am able to anticipate roadblocks, make negotiations and troubleshooting arrangements in advance, and ensure smooth functioning of operations. In turn, this has had a multiplier effect on the rest of the organization. My managers keep me updated on production plans, supply chains, budget shortfalls, factory repairs and expansions for the upcoming year, and so we are able to plan solutions in advance.

ᔐ

It is always a good idea to keep an eye on the future. One need not even be overly ambitious or formulate some kind of rigid mathematical theorem for success. God knows that a million eventualities and unprecedented changes in circumstances can thwart the most well-planned schemes. However, it is good, I would say absolutely *necessary* to have a basic plan. Planning is not about coming up with a tight formula that you mindlessly follow, but about always factoring in the future even when setting a short-term goal. In raising a successful, thriving family and supporting my father's business, my mother built the foundation for our success—not unlike pioneering entrepreneurs and inventors. Smart planning is not limited to any one field, and when applied with dedication and foresight, results in satisfying results for all involved.

3

INVENTORY MANAGEMENT

Rahul is a logistics manager at a toy manufacturing company in Jaipur. Recently the company has been having problems with their stocks. There is no clear picture of inventory costs, he is uncertain about what quantities of supplies and materials they have in stock, and how much to order. As a result, his colleagues are having trouble keeping production on schedule, because they can't get the materials they need on time. Most importantly, orders are not being fulfilled on time because of shortages of parts and equipment.

This is a very common problem. What can one do to fix this? In a native commerce world where small-to-medium businesses compete against global conglomerates, inventory management is key for an efficient supply chain and a healthy business. Managing inventory includes aspects such as controlling and overseeing purchases—from suppliers as well as customers—maintaining stock, controlling the amount of product for sale, and order fulfilment.

Some common-sense measures for managing inventory efficiently are:

1) Consolidating distribution networks, in case your product is stocked in locations where there is not much demand, i.e. moving stock from low demand areas to higher demand locations, thereby optimizing on warehousing and transportation costs.

2) Reducing supply lot sizes, i.e. ordering or supplying fewer products at one time or producing them more frequently, in accordance with the constantly evolving demand and supply.

3) And most importantly, well organized inventory tracking and analysis is critical in ensuring that customers get the goods they need when they need them and that the shelves are adequately stocked.

٢

Now consider another scenario. The lady of the house is planning an elaborate dinner for her husband's biggest client, who is coming over with his family. The spread she has planned is impressive, spanning multiple cuisines, varying from north Indian to continental, with some rounds of dessert too. She is making preparations with the house help Laxmi in the afternoon, when suddenly her brother-in-law, her husband's closest brother, drops by the house unannounced. Apparently, he is in town for a business trip. Now she has to pause dinner preparations, welcome her brother-in-law, and host him over tea with some snacks to go along with it, of course! The man realizes his poor timing and suggests going to a hotel instead, but his Bhabhi will not hear of it. She knows his favourite tea-time snack is *poha*, and he happens to be the only one in their extended family that enjoys it. Do you think the woman was 'out of stock' and unable to fulfil his simple craving? Not on her watch! She asks Laxmi to run to the pantry and grab a fresh packet, which she had bought for just such an occasion. Meanwhile she cuts onions, potatoes, plucks curry leaves from the garden and whips up the delicious, healthy snack in no time.

Having enjoyed this treat, the man wishes to get a shave before dinner. He goes to his Bhabhi to ask if there is an extra razor and shaving cream. Of course, there is! Post-shave and after a relaxing bath, the man finds fresh towels laid out for him. He hadn't even asked for them but the woman of the house made sure they were waiting for him.

She has thought of every eventuality and stocked up on all items that anyone may need in the house, at any time. She does her grocery shopping once a week or once in two weeks. She keeps meticulous records of all the ingredients in the kitchen, along with cleaning and other supplies required for the maintenance of the house and its occupants. When an ingredient or essential runs out, it is immediately noted down. Before she or her husband go shopping, she checks if anything is running out and adds it to their list. A separate whiteboard is hung outside the kitchen for the rest of the family, where the husband and kids add any personal items that they need, every week. All supplies are restocked at the beginning of the month, while other miscellaneous items and groceries are replenished every week or so, from either the neighbourhood grocer or the large supermarket a bit further away. The idea is to economize and make each trip count.

She knows where each and every thing is kept in the house. Family members and guests, used to being looked after like royalty in the house, go to her first when in need of anything, be it food, clothes, stationery or grooming items. The woman has a notebook perhaps, to keep track of some things. But mostly, the inventory tracking device is her brain, on which is imprinted the quantities of all goods in the house and all shortages or excesses. She has developed this device after years of experience in running a house and taking care of each member of the family, ever since her marriage. It's debatable whether she actually had much choice in the matter, as social customs for women are rigid and they are expected to shoulder all the domestic and caretaking duties at their in-laws' place. However, to survive and fulfil these responsibilities she has evolved a simple, holistic approach to inventory management.

ٮ

The woman described in the previous section could be any one of the millions of married women in India who are in-charge of their households. Most of them are not trained in any of the prestigious management schools, and yet they are the rockstar managers of their 'enterprises'. Corporates could learn more than a thing or two from these managers. These women are *no* different from my mother, who has over the last six decades starred in her innings as our 'manager'. There has hardly ever been a shortage of anything in our house, be it in terms of food, cleaning, medical or personal supplies. It's a perfectly efficient system.

She thinks of everything. Till date, we have maintained her meticulous system for storing and growing our own foodgrains. When our new kitchen was built, she made sure to factor in storage space for grains. We can store up to 5 kilogrammes at a time. For other essentials like spices she always has reserves, which are constantly replenished. In the pandemic world of 2021, with frequent lockdowns and uncertainty over the availability of essentials and shutting down of markets and supply chains, this piece of forward-looking thinking by my mother is, as I realize now, a priceless blessing. Sure, sometimes the quality varies, but it is mostly standard and now we know what we need to get whenever the pandemic lockdown restrictions are relaxed for some days, when everything might be available. This efficiency is already built into her management approach. We don't have to go running to the shop for every little item, such as the shaving tools in the previous section's example. Our time and energy is not wasted looking for or sourcing these items for everyday living.

Good inventory management is the cornerstone for a relaxed and content household. From our childhood, dad and mum knew we were fond of sauces and cheese and jams, so when they went shopping they made sure to buy these in abundance. Instead of the small bottle of jam they bought the bigger 1 kg bottle, for sauces they always got the pack of 6 bottles together—so they didn't have run to the shop every time we finished one. Unbeknownst to us, my mother had already factored in the calculations when it came to items like jam or shampoo—a bottle of shampoo costs less than the same quantity in sachets. Not just the essentials, but even the other consumables we used had their place on the list, arranged according to our priorities. We wrote on writing pads throughout our childhood, teenage and even later years, so they ordered pads, pencils and pens in bulk too. Whatever was required on a regular basis was always bought in sufficient quantities.

Moreover, all the items which were stocked or ordered frequently were used up, mother made sure of it. There was no wastage or stocking up of unnecessary, infrequently used perishable items. In fact, most of our shopping for clothes, cricket bats, Kashmiri carpets, new suits for Diwali used to happen at the annual Numaish, or sports fair, held in Aligarh. We had to make our clothes and toys last until the fair came around in January every year. We couldn't buy anything new in between. Further, my mother never ordered miscellaneous items that she was unsure of. Only the essential edible, hygiene, cleaning and stationery items were maintained in stock. This way storage space and purchasing costs were saved, not wasted. Overstocking is a common problem faced by businesses, resulting in blocking of cash flow and warehouse maintenance, storage and labour expenses. For instance, the fear of price hikes in raw materials induces business to overstock. However, we were taught to buy stocks enough only for planned production—raw materials should never be speculated with, as the cost of production goes up with storage, etc. This problem we were able to completely avoid owing to mother's hawk-eyed oversight of inventory.

∽

Our mother's approach to managing inventory has seeped into my own management approach at the office. For instance, I make sure we are always stocked up on the so-called 'low-value' office items, without worrying too much about costs. Even if these things lay around for two years, their cost is negligible. But if a little extra screw costing a rupee can prop up a door handle worth ₹2,000, isn't that way more valuable than saving a few rupees here and there? For example, if you need 2,000 door handles and 2,000 screws, then you calculate: the screws, even if they lie around unused, are worth less than 10% of your total cost (of door handles). If you lose a box of screws, you can't do anything with the handles! So we order screws for 6 months. And when we buy them in bulk, we save a lot of money too. But you can't always calculate these savings in terms of money alone. Sometimes convenience and availability are far more important, for something to be there in hand is more valuable than the effort involved in repeatedly sourcing them or cutting monetary costs.

⌢

Improvisation was a big part of my mother's inventory management, which has taught me its importance not only at home, but in business too. If the house help had forgotten to notify her of some ingredient or the other running out, she would improvise! If we ran out of sprinkles, she would substitute with ground nuts. If we ran out of gum, she showed us how to use mashed rice to stick paper for our school projects. If one of us children refused to eat something, she would innovate—tweaking the recipe by adding something which would immediately make the dish irresistible. For instance, when serving methi, which is very bitter, she would drop in a spoon of honey and we would devour it.

An important part of her inventory strategy was the long relationships she nurtured and maintained. Our suppliers for poultry, fish and chicken have been constant for years. Our egg supplier has been with us for 35 years, and we have never received a spoiled egg—only the freshest eggs. Our meat supplier is paid cash on a daily basis, and he sends us the choicest cuts without any hassle. Lasting relationships with suppliers mean that they are always prepared to meet our expectations, leading to mutually beneficial relationships. More than managing inventory, my mother has ensured the best quality of groceries too, by not chopping and haggling over a few pennies. She kept grocers and suppliers happy by giving them regular business even at the cost of a slightly higher premium.

Despite paying a small premium for essential items, it did not increase our overall budget, and this has to do entirely with the efficiency of the supply chains that she had set up and maintained. Since she always planned meals meticulously and supervised shopping for the house, she managed her limited budget flawlessly. She was given a fixed amount by my father, for groceries and other house supplies. In fact, she always managed to save money, like all efficient homemakers!

∿

If you look around the market for inventory management solutions, you will find a number of sophisticated softwares. Some of them are superlative in their scope and function. However, there are no such calibrated instruments available to homemakers like my mother. How then, did she manage to run the show efficiently? Indian homemakers can reel off the approximate quantities available in their 'stock registers', without resorting to computers. Had this mind-boggling talent been transferred to the business world, India and not Japan would have been the inventor of 'just in time' management.

My mother's system is completely manual. She has mastered the art of inventory management just through sheer dedication, hard work and intuition.

⌣

It is from my mother that I learnt to improve inventory targets. Running on a tight leash is counter-intuitive when it comes to inventory and stock: what seems like a cost-efficient measure in the short term will turn out to be a nightmare when it comes to mitigating the domino effect dealt by inventory shortage. For instance, at a time when brass prices were reaching record highs, we bought brass stock for a year. But this was *not* a smart move, as we had to pay interest on excess raw material, which is costlier than rotation of raw material with regular purchasing. A weak link in one supply chain can bring the whole business to a halt. The manager's job, then, is not only to make sure there is enough for the time being, but also prepare for the future, and eventualities. It pays in the long term to cut a comfortable margin when it comes to inventory. It will also allow a vigilant manager to resolve seemingly apparent contradictions between cost and benefit. As the exceptional statistician and quality manager

Genichi Taguchi put it:

'Cost is more important than quality but quality is the best way to reduce cost.'

Till date if my tie is not matching my shoes, she will ask me to go back and change. For her presentation in business is vital.

4

FINANCIAL MANAGEMENT

'Too many people spend money they haven't earned to buy
things they don't want, to impress people they don't like.'

—WILL ROGERS

As there is a certain truth to these words, it becomes
important to understand how to manage our finances
efficiently and effectively. Not just at a personal, individual
level but also at the level of business. For homemakers across
the world, including my mother, managing money was one
of the many skills she perfected while learning to efficiently

run a household, raising children and supporting my father in business and life. Indeed, financial management was one of the key aspects of her success as a 'home manager'.

⌣

But first, let us go through the basics of financial management and its importance in business. Financial management means planning, organizing, directing and controlling financial activities such as procurement and utilization of funds of an organization. It involves applying general management principles to one's financial resources. Its basic objectives are:

1. Maintaining a sufficient supply of funds.
2. Ensuring good returns for investors and incentives for employees.
3. Optimum and efficient utilization of funds.
4. Creating real and safe investment opportunities.
5. Maintaining flexibility in budgets to keep up with changing markets.

In other words, for any business to make money one needs to plan a budget, figure out the best possible use of organizational funds, that is finding the most profitable products or services to sell, investing smartly and minimizing the costs of manufacturing products or providing services—

all the while ensuring the best quality, maintaining a steady cash flow and not letting funds be tied up in excess stocks or wasted on extraneous expenses.

Financial management is a crucial part of running a business and it's important because:

1. It helps in improving the profitability of an organization.
2. It increases the overall value of an organization.
3. It provides economic stability.
4. It encourages employees to save money, which helps them in personal financial planning.

Financial management is equally important in running households, except the main objectives are to increase savings, ensure financial security for family members for their future well-being and contingency funds. Homemakers have perfected the art of saving and getting the most out of a rupee—be it through meticulous budgeting, getting the best grocery deals, discounts, or saving every extra rupee for the future.

In our household we operate by the motto, 'Buy less, but buy the best.' This basically means that household items and groceries are not bought in excess (to avoid wastage) but just the right quantity (reserves included). However, we make sure that we do not compromise on quality, giving top priority to our health, hygiene and convenience. For instance, keeping reserve stocks of any items other than rice, wheat grains and mustard oil would be considered an excess as they are bound to get spoiled and go to waste. Good quality rice such as basmati can be stored for a long time, while some other grains and mustard oil mature well with time.

My mother has taught me that we should maintain at least 10% to 15% flexibility in our budgets. Why? Let's discuss with an example. Let's assume that I have a budget of ₹3,000 per month for clothes, shirts and trousers and such. However, at the clothing store I find that I can actually get four high-quality cotton shirts for ₹4,000, instead of the two I had originally budgeted for. If I do get the four shirts, I would exceed my budget by 33%. But if I buy the two extra shirts, my requirements for the next 2 months will be taken care of, and I will save ₹2,000 next month! So without compromising on quality, I exceed my present budget but save more in the future. This is why budget flexibility is important.

Let us take another example from business. Say I need to replace a tool in one of the factory's machines, and have two options: one is a cheaper tool for ₹3 and the other is 10 times more expensive priced at ₹30. The cheaper option is of inferior quality, while the expensive one is certainly superior. Which one should I pick? If the latter option ensures longer running time then obviously the higher expense is justified. I will be saving money in the long-run, by using the tool without worrying about repairs, proper functioning and disruption in the production. Thus, it is imperative to keep budgets flexible if it can afford greater savings and convenience.

∽

Whatever financial management lessons my mother learned in running our household, she made sure to pass them on to us. This knowledge, passed on either very casually through stories and jokes or as explicit lessons, holds our business and my management in good stead till date.

I remember back when we were children, my mother often handed us money to pay whoever came to work in the house, be it the house help, cook, carpenter, painter or plumber, etc. She would give us instructions like, *The carpenter has worked for two days, give him x amount of money.* Through these situations we understood what average wages were, we also learnt what is an 'advance' and how much is appropriate in what context. For example, if a painter comes to our house and works for three days, I learnt that he can't ask me for an advance of ₹20,000 — that is way out of proportion. He can ask perhaps for ₹500.

Every summer there used to be a mango festival in the main market in Aligarh, which I along with my sisters, eagerly waited for every year. Each month, my mother would give me a fixed amount of money — I was not allowed to go back and ask for more. So, determined to get my money's worth (and of course, being crazy about mangoes!) I learned to figure out roughly how many mangoes I could get for my allowance. That is, I learned to fit the mangoes into my monthly budget, along with all the other treats and necessities I required. As children she always gave us a fixed amount of pocket money. Nothing more, nothing less. We had to make do with what we had, and ration it out to buy whatever we were craving in instalments. If we ran out of money we were not given more, and had to wait for the next month to arrive.

When my sister Arti got married, my younger sister, Prerna, was given the keys to the household and bank locker. My mother's logic was that if they were handed the responsibility, and knew the amount of money in the locker, they would learn to manage our finances. In this way, she delegated responsibility, and taught us financial management through her own methods.

Sometimes I did take risks in the business, against my mother's teachings. Whether it was over-ordering raw material or extended heavy credit to buyers, I was reckless once or twice in my youth. In one instance, a buyer started fleecing us and underpaying after I had extended heavy credit. It was then that I realized I need to be careful, just like my mother has always taught us. If I hadn't realized my mistake, our business would have shut down. But then my mother stepped in, lent her support and urged me to just take one step at a time towards recovery, and I did.

More importantly, my mother made us understand the value of money in other ways. Earlier I used to play cards for money on Diwali. One day, she told me that with the amount of money I could potentially lose, or throw away, I could get one of our employee's daughters married off instead! She said that if I win money in cards it would not make much of a difference to anyone. But there is always the possibility of losing. Instead, if I pledged that money to buy a scooter for an employee's daughter's marriage, she could find a 'better', more desirable family. As a result, that employee would be very grateful and loyal. And such things have actually happened with several employees! *This* is the difference that the Indian style of management brings to the table—compassion. If you infuse your dealings with compassion, in a place like India, you can earn people's loyalty for years to come.

In the past, my mother has financed the education of our managers' children, paying for their tuition at the same school that I attended—the Lady Fatima Higher Secondary School. She has treated all our employees with such compassion that most of them have stayed with us for many years. In fact, most employees have continued to work for us even after crossing the retirement age, at full salary! Through her kindness and compassionate investment, my mother has ensured that we have a dedicated, loyal staff.

But more importantly, she taught us that the value of money lies not in what you have but how you spend it. If you spend on the people around you, rather than on things that you will outgrow or that have temporary use, it will reap much more happiness for others as well as yourself. My mother was alert to the cash flow problems of our domestic worker and other working-class people at our home as well as in the factory. So, she always paid them weekly wages, since they need to buy essential supplies every week. It's difficult to get groceries and other items on credit for the working classes, especially at a time like this when the economy is contracting and there is a cash crunch.

She also paid half of next month's salary to workers by the 25th of every month, instead of waiting for the first week of the new month to pay the entire salary. This way employees got a head start on their expenses for essentials, rent, etc. She also added incentives, but without paying the full salary at one go. In this way, being mindful of the precarious cash flow of the working-class employees, and by staggering their salaries, she kept them motivated while helping them save money. This was a system she evolved over the years in dialogue with the workers, who preferred not receiving all their money at once, for fear of running out too soon.

There is a fascinating local case study in financial management at the eateries in the famous Aligarh Numaish, or the annual fair, which attracts thousands of visitors across Aligarh and outsiders from neighbouring towns and villages. It takes place for about two weeks at the end of winter.

The Numaish holds huge feasts every day—each pandal can feed up to 1,000 people at a time and they are open from 11 in the morning till 2 in the night. They serve all sorts of delicacies like mutton biryani, seekh kebabs, halwa paratha, all varieties of chaats, spiced tea, etc. Besides the food, there are stalls selling handicrafts, textiles and carpets and various cultural events are held.

However, it is the food stalls that are of particular interest and not just because of their heavenly halwa, parathas and tea. It is because of the ingenious financial management system that has been implemented by the hoteliers there. Each establishment occupies a huge tented hall with hundreds of tables. The key role in ensuring smooth operations is played by the waiters or bearers. These bearers are colloquially known as *beras*.

At the start of each day, the owners hand over to each *bera* a set amount in advance. Each *bera* is in-charge of a certain section, like in any other restaurant. As hundreds and thousands of customers throng the tables, the *beras* take their orders and then run around fulfiling them: sourcing rotis, naans, meats and curries for the hungry patrons. There is a vendor for rotis and naans, another for the meat curries, another for the vegetarian curries—each dish has a separate vendor. The *bera* approaches each vendor according to his particular order. He pays for each dish from his advance, and serves his table. At the end, he hands over the final list to the cashier, after collecting and pocketing the total bill. In this way, each vendor is paid separately and immediately and the *bera* himself makes a margin on the final payment—his wages. So, he is incentivized to attract as many customers as possible, to maximize his earnings.

There is no need for tallying, elaborate billing procedures, receipts, or a credit system. This system dispenses with the need for a reception, petty cash, and the entire billing and marketing staff of restaurants. This is a completely decentralized, homegrown system that has been in place for decades. It is a flawless, common-sense approach. The *beras* stand outside the pandals to attract customers, so there's no need to hire other staff! As a young boy, I remember going to the Numaish and identifying the *beras* with the best service and marketing skills and rushing to eat at their pandals.

We have a similar system in our factory where worker wages are paid according to their productivity, i.e. as per the number of pieces manufactured. For example, if a worker makes 10 handles, he gets paid for those 10 handles. Such a system has worked well for us. After a point, other workers started coming in and offering to make 100 handles, instead of the usual output of 40 per day. An incentive-based system increases motivation and productivity. Of course, one should have a baseline and set a fair per-unit compensation, in line with basic costs of living and the ordained minimum wage.

Common-sense management techniques are not only seamless but they reduce overheads. Out-of-the-box thinking is the need of the hour for businesses, especially in these difficult times. My mother has always offered perks for work well done, not only for employees themselves but also for their children—paying their school fees, for instance, along with gifts for festivals like Diwali and so on. She has reinforced the message that, 'If you do more, you will get more.'

∫

Last year, the national lockdown took everyone by surprise, including small and medium business owners. Supply chains collapsed, and with the economy at a standstill, business earnings were affected. This led to large-scale layoffs of daily wage workers as well as salaried professionals, and triggered a wave of migration from cities back to villages.

Amidst this devastation, very few organizations stepped forward, dipping into their contingency funds to rescue their employees by not cutting salaries or laying off workers. One of these organizations was Reliance Industries Ltd (RIL), as Nita Ambani, chairperson of the Reliance Foundation, recently announced in RIL's annual general meeting (AGM). 'We as a people have come together and fought this battle. We did not cut salaries, bonuses, or any other compensation for our employees throughout the Covid situation,' she said at their 44th AGM in June 2021.

I am proud to say, that we too at Allen & Alvan Pvt. Ltd. are part of the select group of businesses that did not forget our employees during this calamity. Given my mother's compassionate approach, it was no surprise that she insisted on paying the salaries of all our house helps as well as factory employees. Already loyal and dedicated to our business, these people have been with us for several years. Having ensured income for their survival during an unforeseen disaster with our contingency funds, we have set another example for Indian and foreign management. Businesses should incorporate such contingency funds to pay salaries of employees even during a temporary lockdown situation. This will enable companies to:

- Improve employees' trust in their employer
- Increase employee loyalty to the company
- Increase productivity through high morale
- Facilitate employee satisfaction
- Build a culture of gratitude
- Increase respect for top management

Thus, including contingency management in the financial management plans of business is crucial. These plans must consider employees and their salaries, and should not be restricted to the continuity of products and services. Compassion is a crucial part of financial management. Keeping people at the heart of business and knowing that the value of money lies in how it is spent, or rather what it can do for the people around us, is the most important lesson.

5

MANAGING PEOPLE

'Management is about persuading people to do things they do not want to do, while leadership is about inspiring people to do things they never thought they could.'

—STEVE JOBS

All human endeavour, through the ages, has required people to work together, and not alone. There is always strength in numbers and as a result, the human race has achieved countless milestones. On one hand we have the legacy of Rome as the cradle of modern civilization. Rome wasn't built by just one person—countless folks gave their blood, sweat and tears to make it the pinnacle of human achievement. While more recently, we have the Industrial Revolution which with the steam engine led to the birth of modern industry and for which millions laboured in dusty coal mines and sooty factories. Even Thomas Edison, the great twentieth-century American inventor, was never alone in his laboratory. He had a vast team of collaborators, with whose help he founded General Electric and more than 200 domestic and international companies, essentially bringing together collaborators including investors, engineers and salespeople with a common goal.

All of this is just to say that when you want to achieve something good and worthwhile, it helps to have more than just a pair of hands. Collaboration has always been important. All of history's most impactful entrepreneurs, from Thomas Edison to Bill Gates, Steve Jobs, or Richard Branson, were able to shape our world not only through their inventions, but by their ability to pull in bright people, to harness their talent, and make new things together. Some people have a vision, and the gift of being able to organize others around them and give direction; while others work under these directions and guidance. So, you *need* good managers or leaders to help achieve your vision. But what, you may ask, is the need for management if you have talented people around you?

We need to know how to manage people because each person is unique with their own personal history, desires and motivations. People are not machines, and different people need to be guided and motivated in different ways. To make new things happen or to 'get things done' one needs to involve them in such a way that they too get what they want, so that they are fulfilled, taken care of and they can bring the best of their abilities to the task at hand. This is the basic principle behind people or 'human resource' management.

People management is a skill that is applicable in almost every field imaginable, be it a school, business, sports, hospital, the government and yes, even the family unit! At the heart of all human enterprise is the people themselves. And therefore people's needs and desires should be at the centre of any undertaking.

⌐

As the legendary entrepreneur Steve Jobs has said, there is a considerable difference between management and leadership. If you want to manage people, you need to be a leader. But being a leader is different from being just a 'manager'. A manager is normally reactive, takes a short-term view, and wants immediate results. He is focused on doing things the right way, by following the conventional procedures and processes. He cares about productivity and getting things done as quickly as possible.

On the other hand, a leader has a long-term vision for the business or his department. A leader aims to inspire and motivate employees while helping them grow and develop their skills. It is the job of a leader to provide continuous support and lead the way for the employees to achieve success.

What could go wrong if people management is ignored, especially in business? A poorly managed team could negatively impact multiple aspects of your business; a properly managed team, on the other hand, can boost company morale, optimize production levels and efficiency, and give your company a competitive advantage in the marketplace. Organizations that have low morale and engagement often have high rates of employee turnover and burnout. Implementing optimal people management strategies can give your employees a strong sense of ownership over their work and improve their overall job satisfaction. Only when a company truly takes care of its people will it become a success.

In the case of small businesses, understanding how to harness the best out of their team can give them an added competitive advantage in the marketplace. According to experts, since small businesses often lack the budget or market presence of their larger, corporate counterparts, maximizing their pool of resources is crucial, and this includes optimizing their human capital and prioritizing teamwork.

⌇

J.R.D. Tata embodied this sound approach of managing people decades before management theory caught up with him. A legendary aviator, entrepreneur and erstwhile chairman of the Tata Group, J.R.D. is best known for founding several industries with Tata Consultancy Services (TCS), Tata Motors, Titan Industries, Tata Salt, Voltas and Air India, among others. In the book *The Joy Achievement: Conversations with J.R.D. Tata* (1995), he shares the secrets of his managerial success.

Admitting that he had no formal training in management when he started out in 1926, he says, '[My] only contribution to management had to be in handling men who had been so trained. Every man has his own way of doing things. To get the best out of them is to let them exploit their own instincts and only intervene when you think they are going wrong.' All his management contributions involved the human aspect of inducing, convincing, and encouraging his colleagues.

Elaborating further on this process he says, 'When I have to make a decision I feel I must first make sure that the superior knowledge of my advisers confirms the soundness of my decision; secondly, that they would execute my decision not reluctantly but by being convinced about it; thirdly, I see myself in Tatas as the leader of a team, who has to weigh the impact of any decision on other Tata companies, on the unity of the group.' He always kept the big picture in mind, rather than wielding absolute power he took a collaborative, deliberative approach by empowering his cohort to think and act for themselves and the organization.

J.R.D. admitted that he had been criticized as well for being too much of a 'consensus man'. 'I am disinclined to take hard decisions because they would create unpleasantness. But I personally feel, though I may be wrong, that keeping a certain constancy in the way people regard you, in the way you relate to people, will result in a good net result over the long-term.' His people-centred management sought to treat employees like family, and was wary of taking strong, hard decisions like firing people indiscriminately, or pitting groups within the organization against another, without considering the human costs.

We see that J.R.D. Tata had an intuitive grasp of people and collaboration, despite no formal management training. He listened to others, treated every individual according to their character in order to draw the best out of them and delegated work to the experts on time.

∿

There are many similarities between J.R.D. Tata's and my mother's approach to management. Whether it is in raising her children, caregiving for the rest of the family, or managing workers in the house and in the factory, people and their well-being have been foremost in her mind for decades. And she picked up this skill herself, through her work, without any training whatsoever.

One of her most important achievements, I think, is that she always gave us a feeling of abundance, throughout our childhood. She never made us feel that we were lacking in anything. Experts in child psychology or developmental psychology will tell you how powerful this feeling is, for children's self-esteem and growth. For instance, Erik Erikson's influential theory on the psychosocial development of human beings posits that a sense of competence motivates the behaviours of each human being at different stages of life.[1] This competence and confidence in their personhood are either fostered by the encouragement and nourishment of parents and teachers (or children who don't receive nourishment from parents tend to doubt their abilities to be confident or successful). If we wanted something sweet, my mother would almost always make sure to get us a dessert—

---

[1] https://www.verywellmind.com/erik-eriksons-stages-of-psychosocial-development-2795740

either a packet of sweets or chocolates; and if there was nothing in the house, she would make something. We never felt deprived. If my sisters and I ever asked for something she would pay attention and listen, our needs were validated. We didn't have to keep requesting for the same thing over and over again. If we told her we needed stationery for our studies or work, it was provided for. Anything from pens, pencils to a comfortable chair. Since our childhood, my mother hasn't stopped being attentive, even now. If her grandchild or her daughter-in-law has expressed that they're fond of something, be it food, a toy or clothes, she will make sure to get it for them. Of course, this was only the case when our demands were reasonable. She kept the fine balance between caregiving and spoiling us.

Our obnoxious demands were not fulfilled. For example, I was allowed to purchase only a limited number of my favourite comic books. Even if one of my friends had 10 Phantom comics, I first had to finish reading mine, and then my mother let me borrow and exchange comics/books with others.

I realize now, many decades later as an adult, how important these 'no's' were from our parents. My father's good friend, Harry uncle, who worked in the construction business in the US, told me a story which has stayed with me. He spoke about how when he was a twenty-four-year-old starting out in his first real estate job, he had all these bright ideas for innovative new projects. Even though his bosses praised his commitment, he could never get his ideas approved. He never understood the reason for this, until years later when he had his own business. A young colleague, to his surprise, came up with a similar construction project that he had conceived all those years ago as an upstart. Harry uncle was extremely excited at first, but as he looked at the plan closely he realized that as the business owner he couldn't justify the risks involved. He found himself rejecting the same innovative plan that he had proposed in the past. It dawned on him that young people are full of great ideas and enthusiasm, but they don't have the responsibility. Responsibility comes when you are in-charge of something and hold power. So, you have to consider the risks involved in each and every decision.

My mother echoed the same message: age and responsibility expand your perspective, and what seems appropriate in your youth may not necessarily seem that way later on in life. Whenever we would demand things and she refused she often said, 'You will understand when you have children of your own.' I do, in fact, understand now.

My mother was extremely attentive to other people's needs too—a trait which I have also picked up. For example, when a domestic worker would casually mention that they had to marry off their daughter, she would immediately make them buy sarees, plan the menu and other wedding arrangements and, most importantly, personally make up for whatever shortfall of funds they had. Similarly with the factory employees, she initiated the policy of allowing advances against pending salaries. Sometimes, these advances were not deducted later on; she ensured the self-respect and dignity of the people working for the house and the business. *This* is what management is all about, isn't it? This attitude is not just restricted to her children, but also for relatives, nephews, nieces, along with employees and domestic workers. She would always have something for relatives who visited, and little sweets and toys for the children. She has always been this way, since she recognizes the role everybody has to play in our lives, as well as the business.

With her own children, besides supervising our studies, mother made bedtime stories a ritual. Though they were presented to us as fun activities, I have come to realize that they were a vital part of our growth and education. Most of those stories, I recall now, taught us some lesson—about kindness, generosity, being careful and so on. At the end of each story, before we went to sleep, she always explained the moral of the story. Then she quizzed us on the same, ensuring our active participation so that they became lifelong lessons. When we were faced with a dilemma or a difficult choice, she taught us to weigh the pros and cons. For example, in one of her most important lessons she taught us to choose our friendships carefully. With people who enriched our lives, who gave as much as they took. Friends who had a good influence on us, on our studies, future plans and overall social education. Some of my long-lasting friendships, ones which have continued through so many decades up till now, have blossomed because of my mother's guidance.

She was careful in shielding us from unfair criticism, which can be psychologically damaging at a young age. Even my father, along with my mother, never scolded or ridiculed us in public if we ever made a mistake. He would usually laugh it off in front of outsiders. Our parents always supported us in this way. If we did actually slip up or make an error, they would immediately tell us what we had done wrong within hours or a day, but privately. We were never made fun of publicly. Instead of scolding us directly, my father's approach was to recite a *sher* or poem, which was invariably so beautiful and profound that it left a lasting impression on us.

Using the same principle in the workplace, I make sure that we monitor the factory operations carefully and if there's a quality issue it is immediately flagged. The problem is rectified smoothly, whether it has to do with machinery or any employee. It is communicated clearly, without undue harshness and humiliation. Immediate communication and redressal are key, along with reinforcing confidence in the workers by giving them the benefit of the doubt. This has led to a remarkably efficient staff over the years and we've rarely had any personnel or performance issues. In case of any operation roadblocks the worker is not penalized, blamed or criticized, only those who need to know are told about the problem in a solution-oriented approach.

Our parents had a very safe and nurturing system of expressing their pride in us. Picture this typical scenario from social gatherings with other parents or family: if somebody else is mocking your children, even good-naturedly, your parents also end up participating. People don't realize that it is harmful for their children to see their own parents mocking them.

Also, in such gatherings, my mother would never let any of her three children be compared to others. This too is a common scene: when a smarter boy comes along and parents start saying, 'Oh look at *him*'. Even if somebody's child had accomplished something remarkable, mum would never allow that to reflect badly on us. She would always say something to the tune of: *Chalo, they have done well, no problem. There are other things to do.* Even if my father said, *Look at xyz, they should learn from them and do as well as they have*, our mother would brush it aside saying, *It's fine,*

Wedding photo

On the family horse

In the home garden

With her husband preparing for sister-in-law's wedding

Laying the foundation of temple with Padmashri awardee
Dr J.M. Pawa, a prominent eye surgeon

In the Mussoorie house

Inaugurating a gausala (cowshed) at Aligarh

With nephew Aditya Puri, former Managing Director, HDFC Bank

At her friend's house in Agra

At the Mahakumbh in Allahabad

Inaugurating the gate of the Ramleela grounds dedicated to her husband, the late Devinder Jit Vadra

Celebrating her birthday with the family

Inaugurating an Inner Wheel Club project

Addressing the Inner Wheel Club

Addressing a gathering of the Ladies Club, Aligarh

At a family event

With her nephew Ravi Marwaha (former Vice-President, IBM International) and his wife Alka

At a family wedding wih Prem Chopra and Prem Krishna

In her office

Lunch with friends

With her children and grandchildren

but my kids are doing well. As a result, our confidence levels never dipped and we never envied others or tried to imitate them, thinking there was something lacking in us. Our heads were held high throughout, our self-esteem was nurtured. Whenever she was confronted with others' achievements, she'd tell us: *You have other qualities, and you are adored in this house regardless.* So, we didn't grow up anxious about how others were doing, or uselessly competing with them, just to impress our parents or outsiders.

⌒

With respect to employees, our mother taught us to be compassionate, not just financially, but in our daily interactions and recognizing the dignity of labour of all the people who help run our house and business. I remember when one of our cooks had to go to his native village for a family event, my mother financed his trip home; and when he returned he took leave for another two months—whatever problems he was having he did not communicate them to us. But my mother still paid his salary, assuming that he was probably going through some difficulty (and even if he was not, not receiving salary does not help, especially for the working classes). Even when he decided to quit his job altogether, my mother was not offended. When I asked her why she didn't confront the man she said, 'If you can donate to the Prime Minister's fund why not do this, pay a man his salary?'

Though the cook eventually left, it was not because he was unhappy working for us. When you look after your employees and what they need, they are attached to you. It inspires not only loyalty, but more interestingly, it increases their productivity. You don't need to work on motivating them separately, they are always motivated, knowing that they are being taken care of.

My father once told me a story. It was about a Nawab, his fighter cock and his Munshi, or advisor. When the cock lost its cockfight, the Nawab was furious about losing face and money. So, the Munshi said to the Nawab, 'Your Majesty, I'll get this cock cut up, cooked and serve it to you.' But when the cock started fighting again and won, the Munshi turned around and said, 'Your Majesty, I shall get a gold chain made for it.'

A man in the audience standing next to them was perplexed. He said to the Munshi, 'You're an interesting fellow. One minute you're having the cock killed, and the next you're getting a gold chain made for it?'

The Munshi smiled. 'I'm employed by the Nawab, not the cock.'

My father was trying to tell me that one should inspire

this kind of loyalty from employees. In material terms, this involved paying competitive salaries, along with other benefits. For example, when an employee chose not to invest in the provident fund, we invested both their share as well as ours. So now many of them rake in lakhs of rupees. My last manager got ₹18 lakh out of his PF without investing a single rupee himself! Besides official compensation, my mother has taught me to go the extra mile.

All my manager's kids were or are enrolled in the same school I went to—Lady Fatima Higher Secondary School. My mother has always said, '*Inko padhao* (get them educated).' Following her advice, I did! I paid for their education throughout. And mind you, these schools are not easy to get into. But as an 'old boy' or alumnus of the school I could help. There was a recent instance with a young manager who came to me and said, 'I've applied for my son's admission in Lady Fatima.' I knew that the school usually admits around 200 students out of a total of 2,000 applications, roughly speaking. So, I went and spoke to the principal, she was called 'Mother'. She was my teacher all those years ago. I went to her and said, 'Mother, I'm paying for this boy, is there any way he can get admission here?'

Eventually that boy was admitted. The day after the results came out, my manager came to me with tears of joy and a box of laddoos saying, 'My wife is so happy'. He was gushing with gratitude. 'I would pass Lady Fatima every day when I was young, but I couldn't afford to go there. So, I would dream that my son would get to study there. But even for him admission seemed so difficult, almost impossible! *Aur aapne aise hi kara diya mera kaam....* It was always my dream and you have made it come true,' he said.

This is more than enough gratitude to earn lifelong loyalty, which also boosts overall morale in the workplace. I must admit that I did wonder initially: Why should I make the effort? Why should I bother helping this person? But I remembered my mother's teachings, i.e. it is natural for us to help those around us, those in need, in any way we can and it will come back to us ten-fold. And so, I have been paying that child's school fees.

I remember another incident when one of my former managers, he's retired now, had come to the house. His kid had just passed commerce in school. My mother said, 'MBA *karao.*' I told my mother privately, 'Mummy, so I have to pay now because MBA needs capitation fees!' She just said, 'Do it.' And that was that. I helped that child get admission in the MBA programme in a college in Meerut. I paid the capitation fees, I paid for the books, so he could study for the entrance exam. He got in eventually and graduated. Later, when he was applying for a job at HDFC bank, I could see that with the MBA, he had the necessary confidence. Now he is a circle manager at HDFC.

⟡

Our mother was not just a manager. She was a leader who brought out the best in everyone around us through compassion and positive reinforcement. She also sent employees gifts for important occasions, such as for their children's marriages. She would gift clothes if the daughter was to be married...or whatever else the family wanted for the wedding. We also had a small tradition at home: every year on my father's birthday, for the last 50 years, we have provided employees with dresses of their choice. Whatever they want—be it shirts, matching trousers and so on—they get it. And they keep these clothes and wear them whenever they have to go on social engagements.

We have maintained these small traditions for certain occasions. They could've been discontinued if my mother decided that we should 'save money'. But she encouraged us to be generous, treating employees with dignity. Not as part of the family exactly, but with respect, recognition and appreciation for their labour. Though there are some employees, very old ones who have seen my kids grow up, who have become part of the family over the years.

I have learned to practise compassion from my mother in

these different ways. Even small gestures go a long way. One of my staff members is fond of tea, so I make sure to get it prepared for him, and for the other employees too obviously. I know the time of the day when he is on his break and I know that he's also fond of a particular sweet. So I make sure to send it for him every other day. These small gestures are both made and received with pleasure.

We own a cinema hall in Aligarh. Whenever one of our managers visits the place with family or friends, I inform the staff to treat them like VIPs. They are served the best snacks, given the best seats—top-notch hospitality all around. All this for free. Money isn't everything, people should feel happy and cared for. Especially people who are part of your business and play key roles in your organization. When it comes to inspiring loyalty in management, money takes a backseat.

I also make it a point to attend weddings and other family functions of employees. I end up financing these events partially if they want to host them in the nearby guest house and they can't afford it. In such cases I tell them, 'It's fine, just do it in the guest house, don't worry.' It's a huge thrill for them, and me, to see that we can be so important in their lives. I take our entire family to these functions, and we all enjoy ourselves.

Once, I remember, I promised a young man working for us that I would attend his wedding. But on the day of the event, I was working late in the factory and forgot all about it. So the senior members in his community came to the factory and told me that the wedding had been stopped! The groom was standing on the rooftop and refused to come down. I had to drop everything, get in the car and rush to the pandal. I climbed up three flights of stairs and finally managed to bring him down! The boy said, 'I want to get my photo clicked with you and now I will!' Everyone was happy, it was a beautiful moment.

‸

My parents' protective, nurturing habits percolated into their dealings in business as well. When bank managers used to come for meetings with my dad, he would scold them about this and that. But when they came with their superiors, for example if the branch manager came with the regional manager, my father would be all praises for the former. He never criticized someone to get them in trouble. He used to say, 'I will tell you that you are wrong when you are with me, alone. But in front of everybody I will always point out your good values.' So, most of the bank managers who worked with us got promoted to higher posts. More significantly, they were efficient in their dealings with us, and our working relationship was forever smooth. In fact, they were happy to bring in their superiors. When these people eventually got promoted to higher posts, they were loyal beyond compare. If they received anything signed by dad or even me now, as I picked up this trait, they didn't have to even look at the letter. 'Just do it,' they'd tell their juniors. We have rarely had any problems with our banking.

Even out in the market, whenever my dad placed verbal orders for anything, it was fulfilled to the T, because he always stood by his word. He commanded respect and loyalty. This is what I learnt and now I get the same response in my own dealings. It actually makes business easy when the people you deal with are treated well. This is the hallmark of a compassionate leader, sound manager and successful entrepreneur.

∿

Whether you are running a household, a school, a small business or a large corporation, you need people to help you achieve your goals. For the people to help you do that, you need to be attentive to their desires and motivations. The best way to do that is to treat them as human beings and treat them with compassion, compensate them fairly, and go out of your way to make them feel appreciated. How can you do that?

You can pay their salaries on time, provide benefits, occasional gifts for their families, empower them by involvement in decision-making, letting them have a voice, avoid direct criticism and punitive action, correct them in private. Maintain positive relations, above all. Positivity does not mean doing away with critical thinking. Criticism should definitely have a place in this, along with kindness. But you don't need an MBA to know that treating people well empowers them and helps you get the best out of them. My mother is a shining example of this approach, and I am grateful to her for teaching it to me.

EPILOGUE

*'There is nothing that can't be done. If you can't
make something, it's because you haven't
tried hard enough.'*

—SAKICHI TOYODA

Homemaking is noble work, and homemakers are the personification of grace, love and dignity. They nourish and hold together not just a house but a family. They turn houses into homes. They take care of not just the immediate family, but each and every member—be it children, spouses, in-laws or relatives—personally. Most importantly, homemaking is not just selfless, noble charity;

it is a skilled form of labour and a sophisticated form of management based on a simple, practical approach.

In this book I have attempted to show, with examples, how running a house is no less than managing a business, and how homemakers like my mother make top-notch managers. Given the enormous success of our family business and how my siblings and I have settled well in life, it must be clear by now that my mother's management skills, and of Indian homemakers in general, are on par with the best managers and entrepreneurs. It is high time that we recognize their labour and skills as such. What's even more impressive is that Indian women homemakers have developed these skills without any formal training or fancy MBAs. Women like my mother gracefully took on the role given to them—that of managing each and every aspect of their household—along with the physical and emotional sustenance of each and every member of the family. They learned on the job, adapted and built efficient operations through a simple, practical approach and common-sense techniques.

Every day, all over India, women wake up early, prepare meals for their children and husband, make sure their clothes are washed and ironed, and that everyone is nourished and ready to take on the world—whether it is for school or the workplace. Working-class women have to do all of this work and then go to their own jobs in other homes, offices and factories. In case of middle- and upper middle-class homemakers with domestic staff, the former have the added responsibility of delegating work, issuing instructions, supervising and quality control. The work of homemakers is ultimately geared towards the well-being of the family, so they have to come up with straightforward, practical solutions to all the long- and short-term obstacles between them and their family's prosperity. Driven by their unconditional love, these women employ everyday common-sense techniques to manage the financial, logistical, social and emotional aspects of the household with finesse.

ᔓ

My mother raised three children—taking care of our education, health and our emotional and physical needs. She was a pillar of strength for my father, who founded one of India's largest private hardware manufacturers. She managed a huge household with children, servants, a workaholic husband, while being the caregiver for in-laws and ensuring top-notch hospitality for the constant flow of guests. And she did all of this always with a smile. She practised and perfected 'management with a heart'. And she taught us the same skills as well!

Women have helmed the Indian household and managed

its myriad responsibilities without any formal training for generations. Their crucial role should be even more obvious now, more than a year-and-a-half into the pandemic, when everyone has been stuck at home. In the pandemic women, mothers have selflessly taken on the additional burden of housework, extra meals and managing spouses and children's needs round-the-clock. In addition to their earlier workload, mothers are now supervising and managing their children's online classes, uploading their homework, ensuring attendance, functioning of computers and internet, homeschooling, sufficient physical and extra-curricular activities and so on. They work twenty-four hours, seven days a week, 365 days a year without any days off or salary. Studies have confirmed that the additional workload brought on by the pandemic has unsurprisingly been thrust on women.

But they have risen to the occasion, and how! Mothers have managed the additional schooling, extra-curricular activities, and in the absence of domestic help, cleaners and cooks, single-handedly kept their families fed, clothed and thriving. This is no small feat, and deserves further study of their work ethic and management techniques. But one thing we know for sure is that they were able to step up only because of their humane values, compassion, sharp eye for details, planning, and exemplary time and financial management.

✓

In conclusion, it would be fair to say that my mother's management style is not unlike the famous 5S system, pioneered by Toyota and other Japanese manufacturers with an additional secret ingredient—a heart. Most industries are able to implement this system after a lot of training, but she has mastered and adapted it to perfection over the years. Let us look at how she has managed to make the 5S system work:

- **Sort:** The first step of 5S, it requires sorting through materials and keeping only the essential items for completing tasks at hand. All other items are to be removed from the work area. This is clear in the way my mother organizes the preparation of meals, with only the most frequently used or necessary items taken out of drawers and shelves, including utensils, ingredients, etc. This also applies to her general approach to work: the most important tasks are completed first and then she moves to the less pressing ones, everything is done in order of priority. For example, when we were young, her first task of the day was to prepare our nutritious breakfast before sending us off to school. Only after this, she moved on to the other tasks.

- **Set in order:** Ensure that all items are organized and

each item has a designated place. Organize all the items left in the workplace in a logical way so they make tasks easier for workers to complete. My mother has made sure this step is followed religiously in our household: as is clear from the way the kitchen is organized, with the heavily used items stored within easy reach. For our newly-constructed kitchen, she made sure to provide storage space for grains of up to 5 kg while other essential spices are always kept in stock.

- **Shine:** Proactive efforts to keep workplace areas clean and orderly to ensure purpose-driven work. This means cleaning and maintaining the newly organized workspace. While my mother is now too old for the physical labour herself, she supervises all cleaning and maintenance tasks of the house like a hawk, ensuring all cleaning supplies are stocked and household appliances functional. This is crucial since we have always had relatives and friends dropping by our house, and keeping everything clean and functional ensures smooth operations.

- **Standardize:** Create a set of standards for both the organization and processes. In essence, this is where you take the first three S's and make rules for how and when these tasks will be performed. My mother has thoroughly trained our house staff in their responsibilities and respective schedules, including the cook, the cleaner, the gardener and so on. Our grocery, cleaning, meat and fish supplies are always prompt and of top quality, due to long-term working relationships with vendors.

- **Sustain:** Sustain new practices and conduct audits to maintain discipline. This means the previous four S's must be continued over time. This is achieved by developing a sense of self-discipline in employees who will participate in the 5S. Not just our staff, my mother made sure that we, her children, never missed a single day of school and were regular with our schoolwork. This helped me cultivate discipline for school, college and later, business as well. My schedule for production targets, supply deadlines, client interactions and almost every other aspect of business is well planned. In turn, my managers remain on top of things and anticipate any hiccups in production or supply and troubleshoot accordingly.

So, it is clear that my homemaker mother is not only an excellent manager but she has also mastered a few quality management tools, much before they were being formally taught in management schools!

Finally, in addition to the 5S's my mother's secret ingredient is: compassion. Not just for her children, husband or other family members, but also for our household and factory staff, our vendors, meat and poultry suppliers, *kirana* shop owner, temporary construction labour and so on.

It was because of her compassion that she was able to organize her routine and responsibilities around our sustenance. With caregiving as her primary objective, my mother was able to devote quality time for all. Not just for us kids, but my father, our domestic workers as well as factory employees were taken care of, and this meant that they performed well in their jobs and responsibilities. She took care of employees' children's education; paying a part of staff salaries in advance; she always kept in mind gifts for family members, cousins, relatives, workers and employees for important occasions; shielded us from outside criticism; made sure to spend time with us playing, telling stories and sharing life lessons; taught us that the value of money lies in not what you have, but how and where you spend it. And through all this, she taught us to be compassionate towards others.

People and their well-being have been foremost in her mind for decades and she has been a beacon of hope for many with her compassionate leadership. I'm immensely grateful that she has passed down this invaluable quality to me and shaped my own management style. Leaders need to be prepared to put others first, before themselves. This is an essential aspect of 'servant leadership', if we are to speak in corporate terms. She has led by example, and with a heart. And just as I have learned from her, I have tried to pass on these qualities to my managers and employees as well.

An employee takes cues from the manager's actions, whether they are being compassionate, investing time to engage in meaningful conversation with the team, encouraging them to perform their best, being a supportive shoulder when they fail, or inspiring them to perform even better and win together as a team. In leading by example and compassion, raising a successful, thriving family, and supporting my father's business, my mother built the foundation for our success. This model is easily replicable and will prove to be extremely useful for students, managers and corporates.

ACKNOWLEDGEMENTS

I am deeply grateful to my father, the late Mr Devinder Jit Vadra, and my mother Mrs Urmil D.J. Vadra for imparting life's important lessons to me. They have aided my growth and taught me values that have helped me lead a meaningful and successful life, such as kindness, compassion, respect for intelligence and morality, and being a dependable friend. Most importantly, they taught me how to run a business efficiently and successfully—lessons I have tried to outline in this book. This book is for them.

I want to thank my wife Priti, who is my rock and anchor in all my endeavours, and my children, Dhandev and Deven, who are everything a father could ask for—affectionate, respectful, obedient, and high achievers. A big thank you to both my sisters, Arti and Prerna, for their unrelenting support, and my brothers-in-law, Alok Gupta and Vidur Kohli, as well as their families, Kunaal, Nandita, Veer, and Shivani, for their love and respect.

I am also grateful to everyone, family and friends, who were integral to this endeavour, including Shweta Bansal, Dr Professor Tariq Mansoor, Professor Javaid Akther, Professor Parwaiz Talib, Smiley didi, Aditya Puri, Sunil Puri, Atul Pape, Meenu bhabi, Surendra Pape, Ladi Pape, Nona Pape, Avinash Dutta, Neeru, Neelu and Ashok Gulani, Geetanjali, Ramesh mama, Suman mami, Janak masi, Vedi mama, Vibha mami, Aruna mami, Ravi Marwaha and Alka bhabi, Mamta, Rohit, Bittu, Renu, Vijay Puri, Honey, Dimpy, Renu didi, Reshma and Raunak, Rohini didi, Arjun Bhola, Poornima, Iqbal Ahmed Khan and Shaista bhabi, Farhan Ahmed Nizami, Vivek Bansal, Dr Satendra Saxena, Dr Himanshu Garg and Dr Bindu Garg, Dr Vivek Nagia, Dr Rakesh Bhargava, Dr Shahid Jameel, Dr Praveen Varshney, Dr Ankur Singhal, Irfan Beg, Mukesh Jain, Priya, Vijay Soni, Raman, Aashima Malhotra, Jhumroo Mama, Awanish Awasthi, Gagri bhaisaab and Rashmi bhabi, Rati, Shelly Kocher, Siddharth, Surbhi and Raman Mittal, Sonu Nayyar, Nazima Masud, Shahnaz Appa and the family at Hafeez Manzil, and Paytm Founder and my friend Vijay Shekhar Sharma.

I also want to thank Kartikeya Jain for helping me translate my thoughts into words, and Rinku Sharma, who worked tirelessly with me, offering valuable suggestions. My special thanks to Kanishka Gupta, my nephew and a superb literary agent, for his kindness and for imbuing my writing with a sheen. I also thank Dibakar Ghosh of Rupa Publications for publishing this book, and for believing in my story.